Solo Guitar

THE BEATLES

FOR JAZZ GUITAR

Arrangements by Bill LaFleur

ISBN 978-0-7119-3155-8

HAL•LEONARD®
CORPORATION
7777 W. BLUEMOUND RD. P.O. BOX 13819 MILWAUKEE, WI 53213

Visit Hal Leonard Online at
www.halleonard.com

All My Loving

Words and Music by John Lennon and Paul McCartney

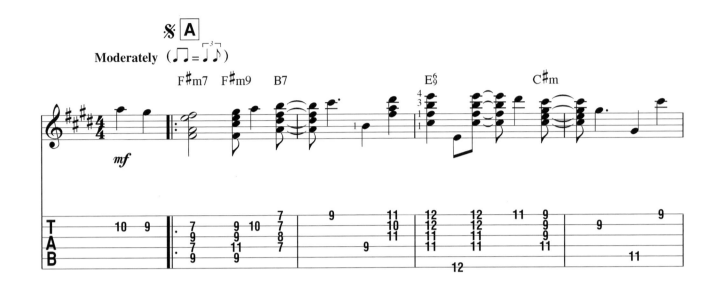

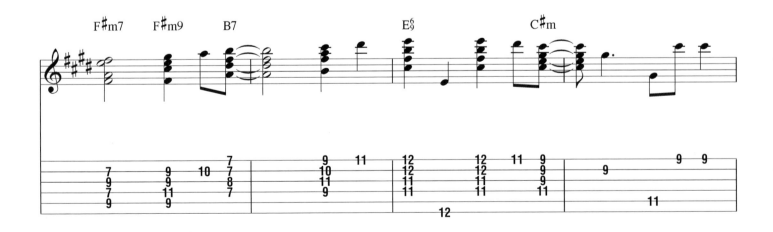

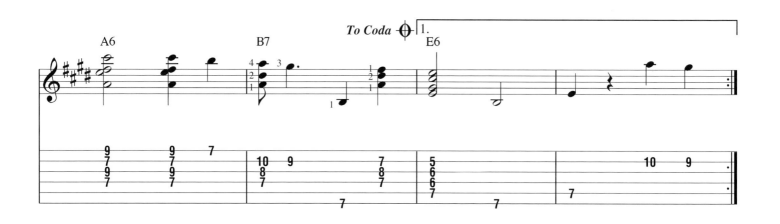

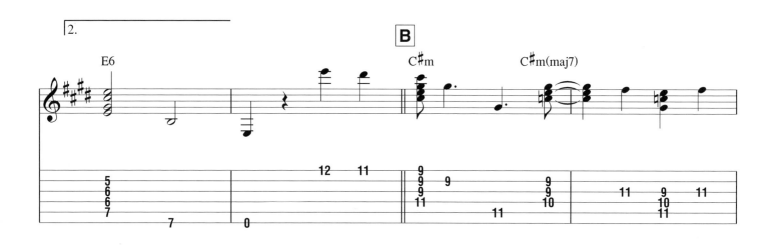

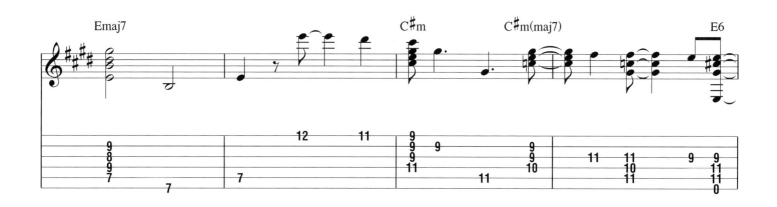

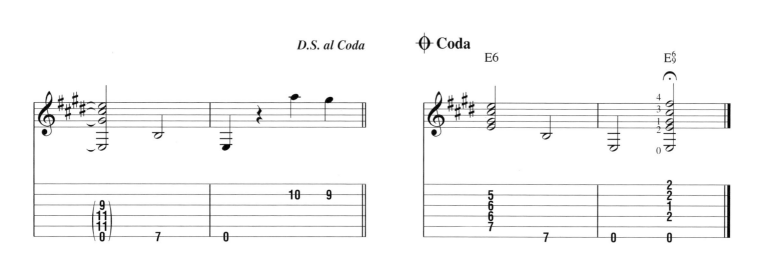

Blackbird

Words and Music by John Lennon and Paul McCartney

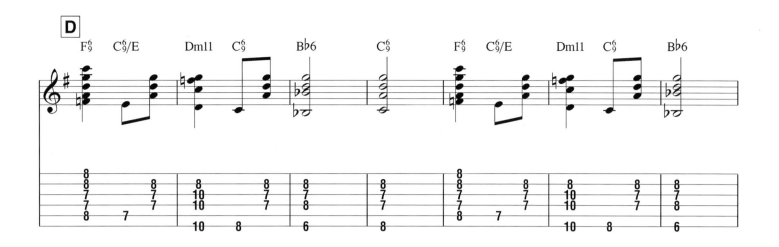

D.S. al Coda

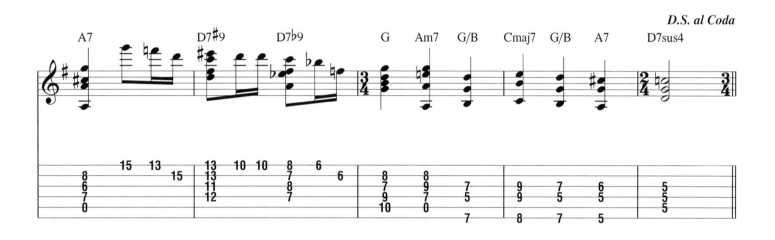

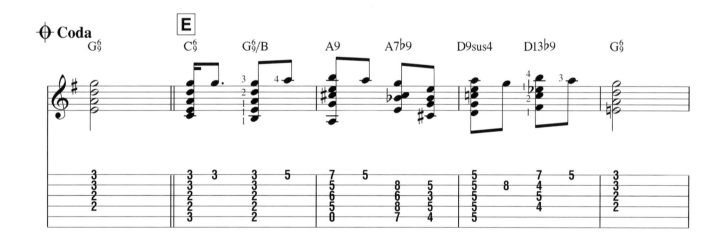

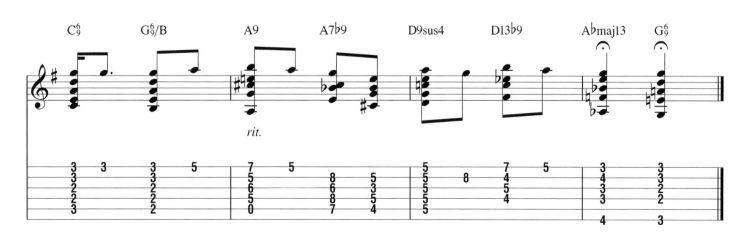

Can't Buy Me Love

Words and Music by John Lennon and Paul McCartney

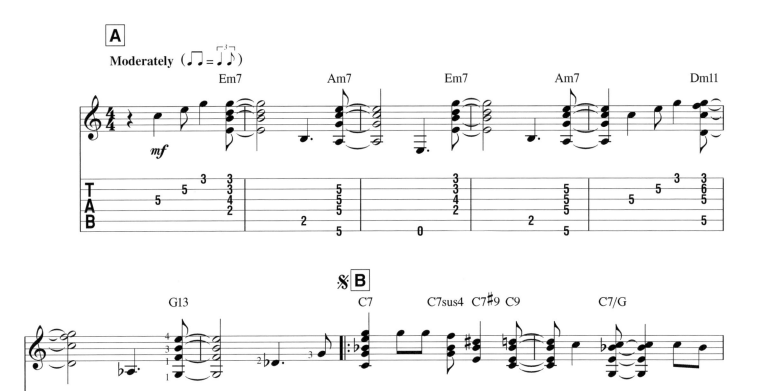

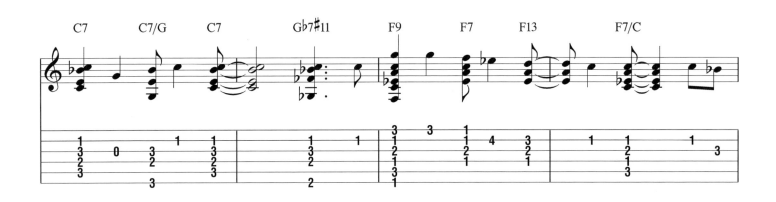

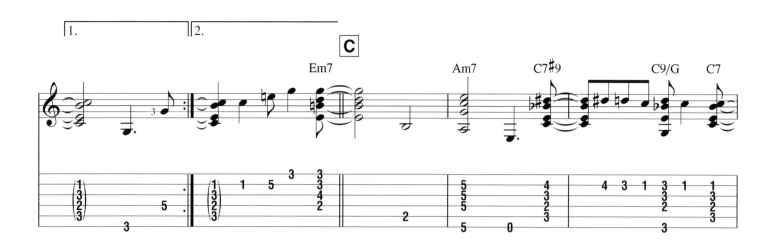

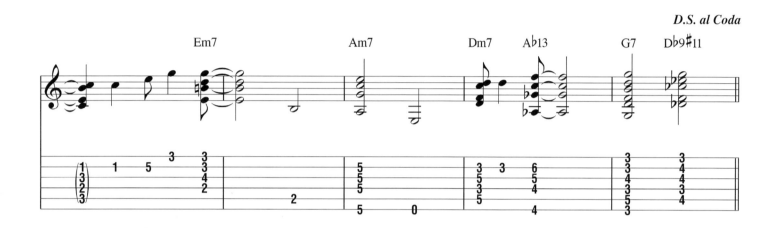

D.S. al Coda

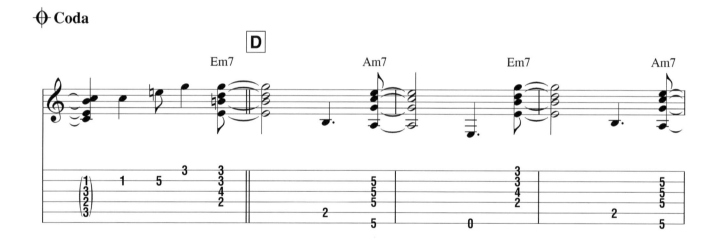

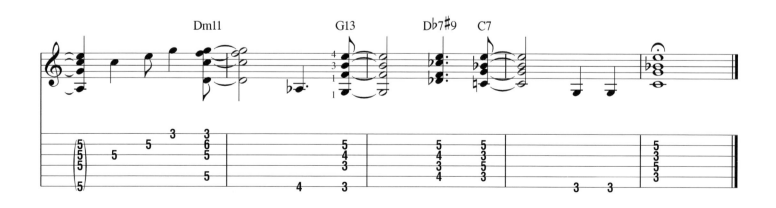

Eight Days a Week

Words and Music by John Lennon and Paul McCartney

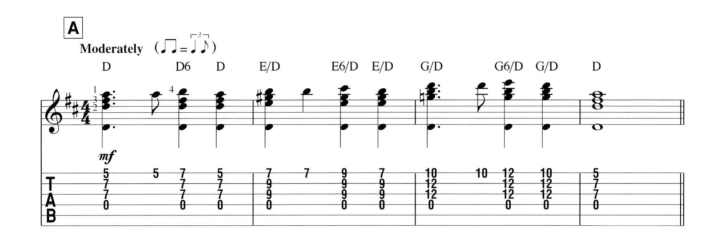

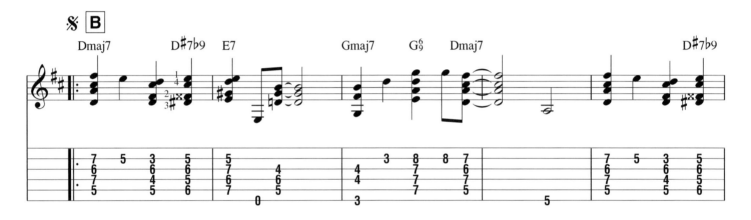

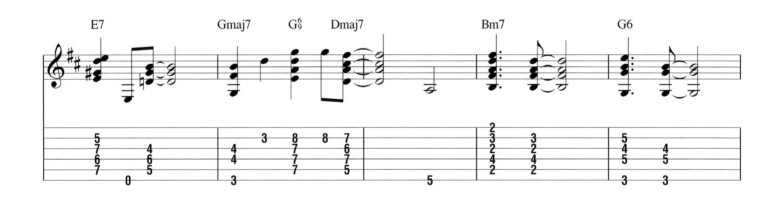

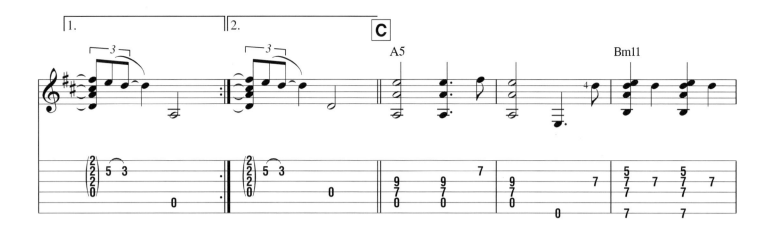

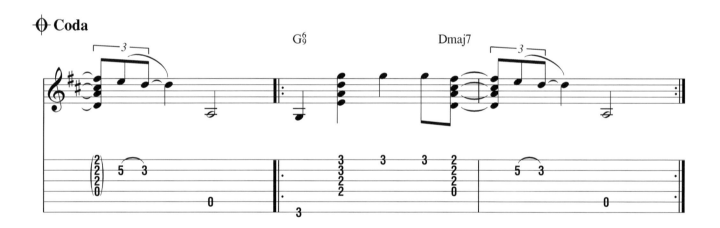

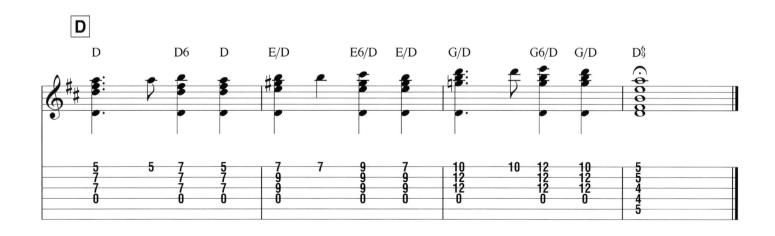

Eleanor Rigby

Words and Music by John Lennon and Paul McCartney

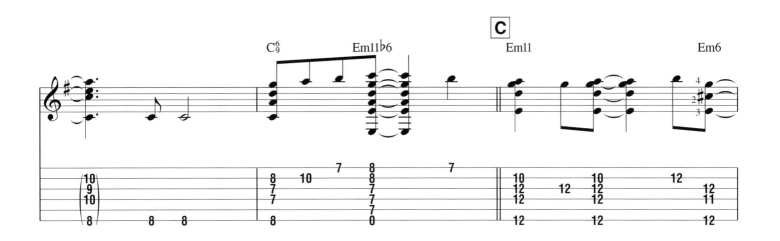

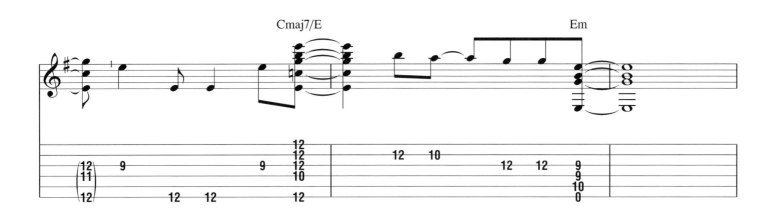

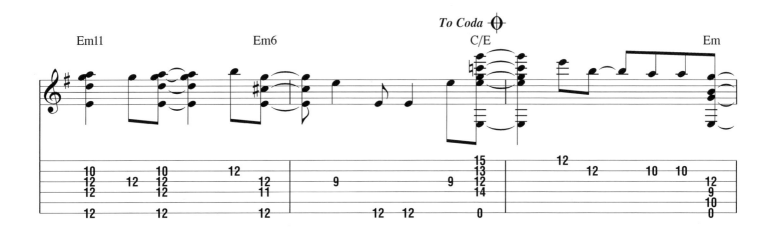

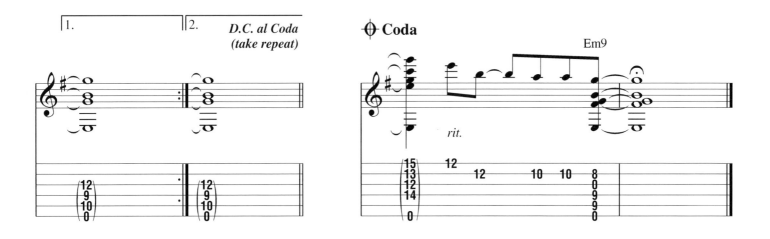

Golden Slumbers

Words and Music by John Lennon and Paul McCartney

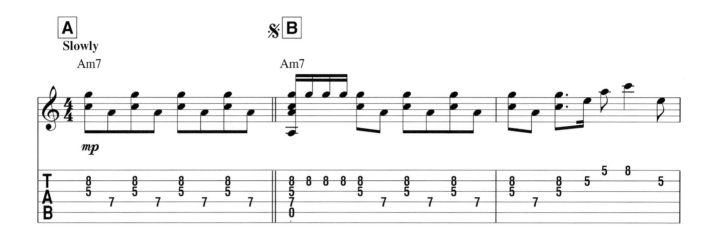

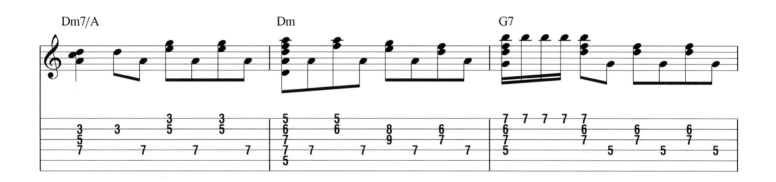

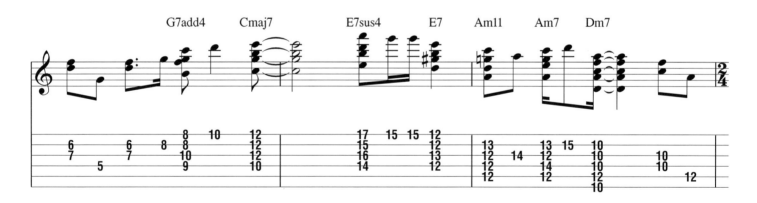

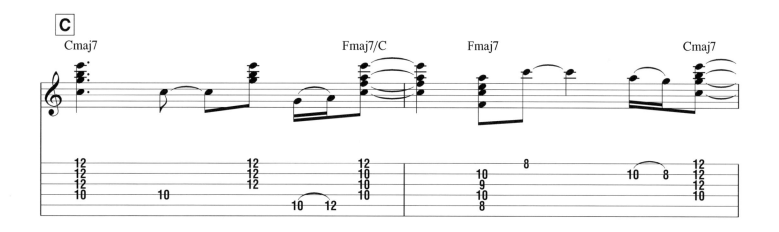

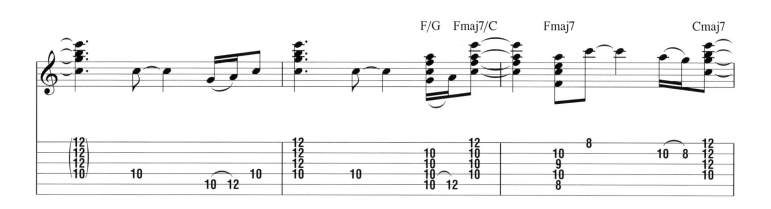

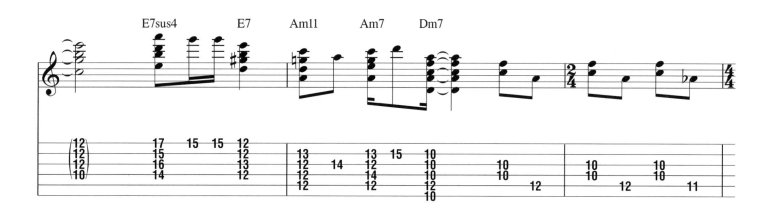

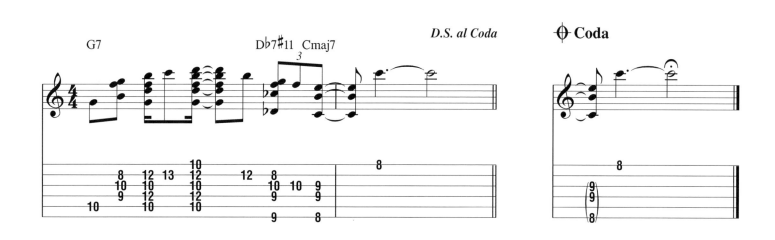

Here, There and Everywhere

Words and Music by John Lennon and Paul McCartney

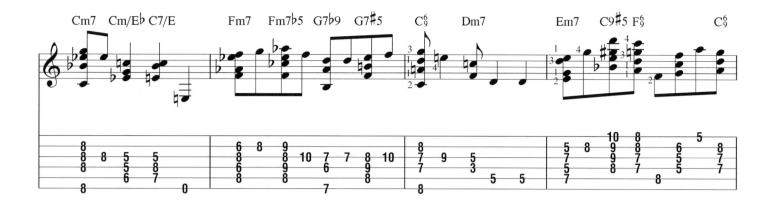

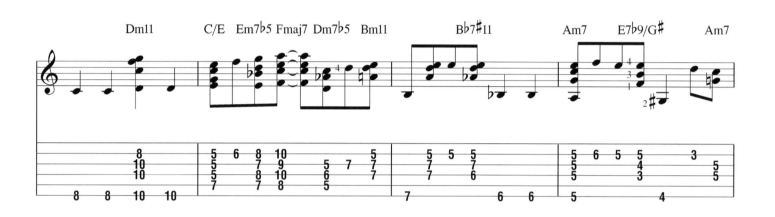

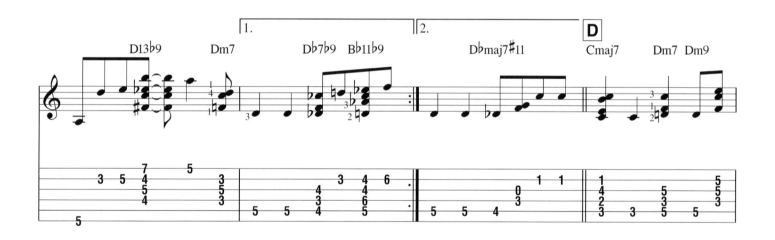

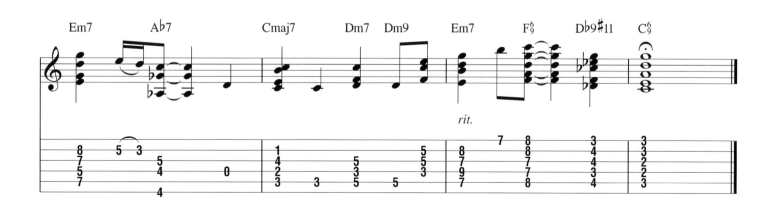

Hey Jude

Words and Music by John Lennon and Paul McCartney

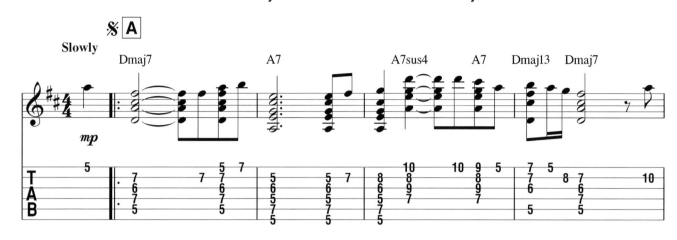

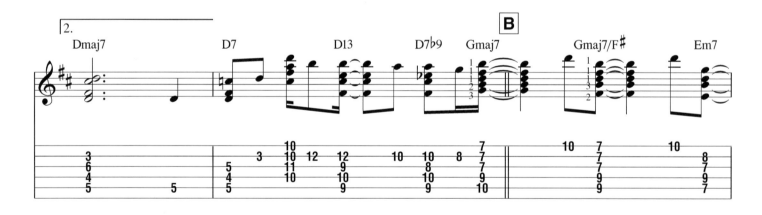

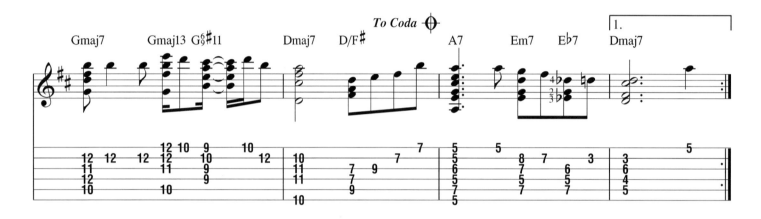

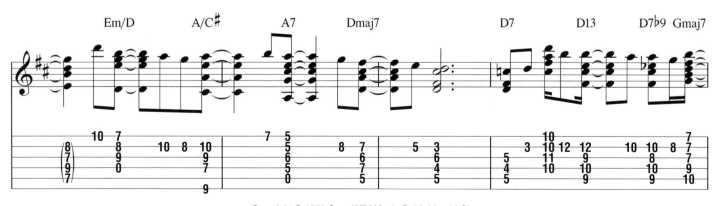

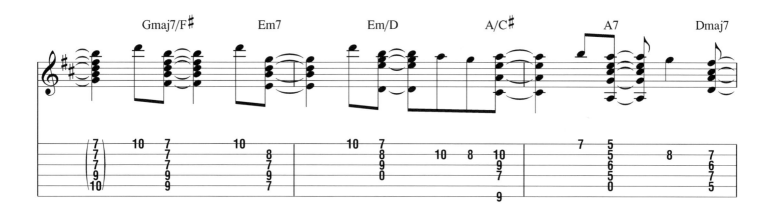

D.S. al Coda

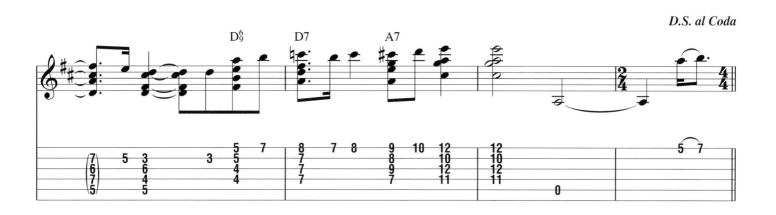

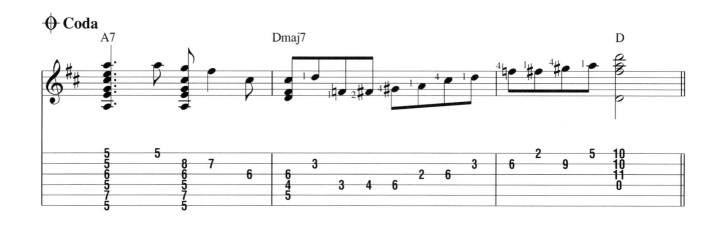

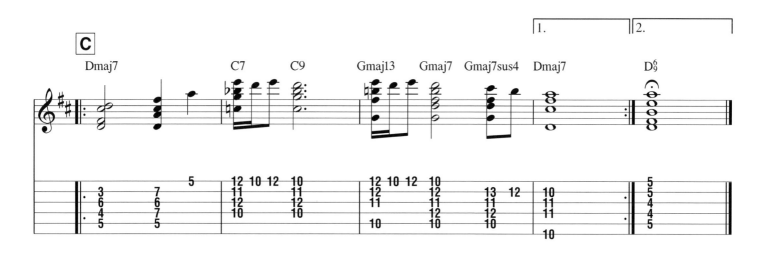

Good Night

Words and Music by John Lennon and Paul McCartney

I Will

Words and Music by John Lennon and Paul McCartney

In My Life

Words and Music by John Lennon and Paul McCartney

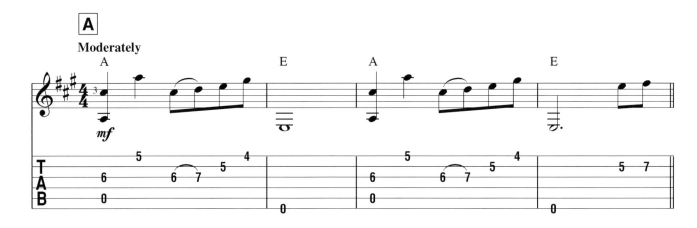

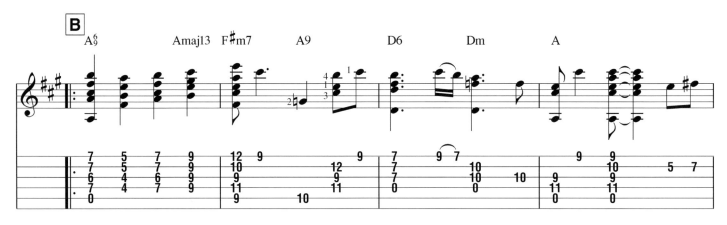

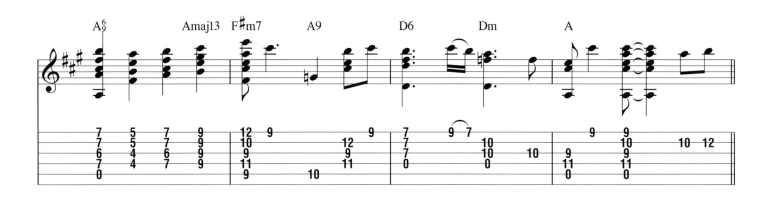

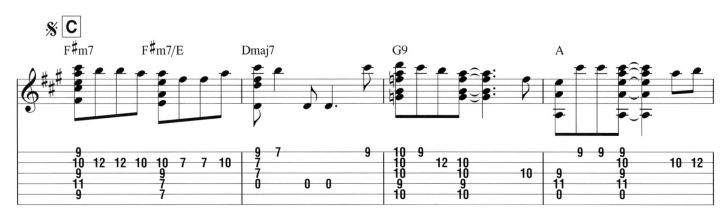

Let It Be

Words and Music by John Lennon and Paul McCartney

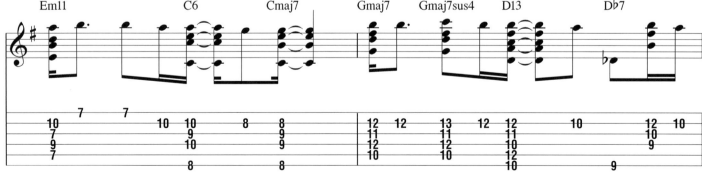

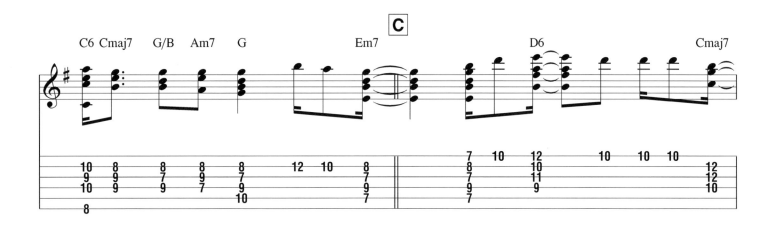

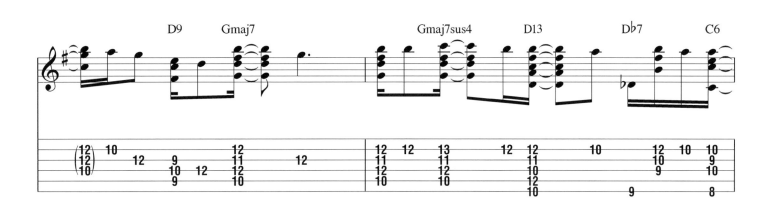

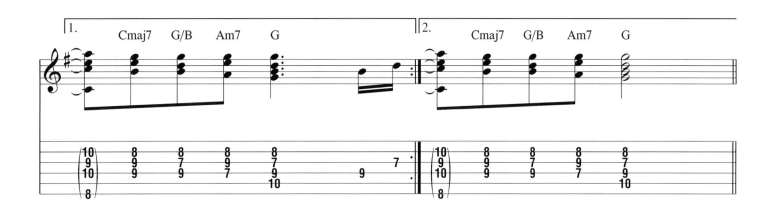

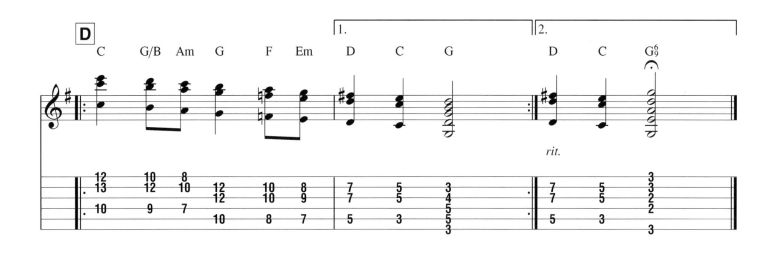

The Long and Winding Road

Words and Music by John Lennon and Paul McCartney

Lucy in the Sky with Diamonds

Words and Music by John Lennon and Paul McCartney

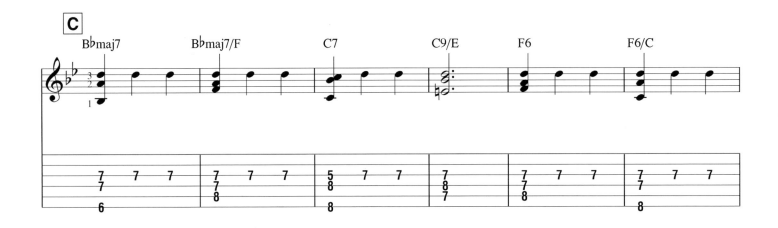

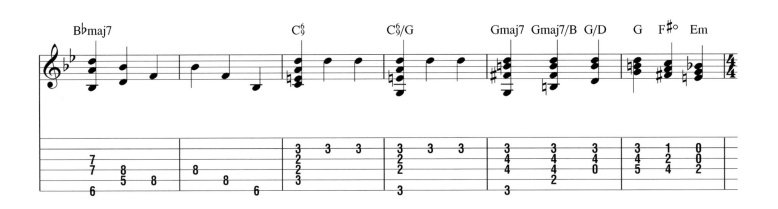

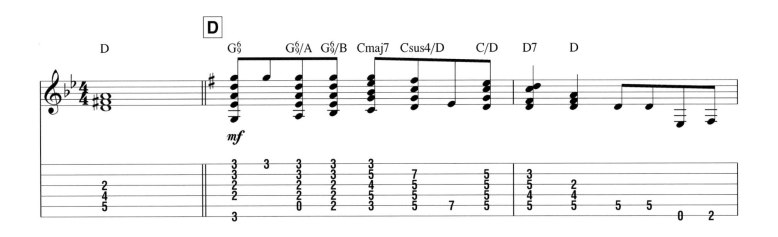

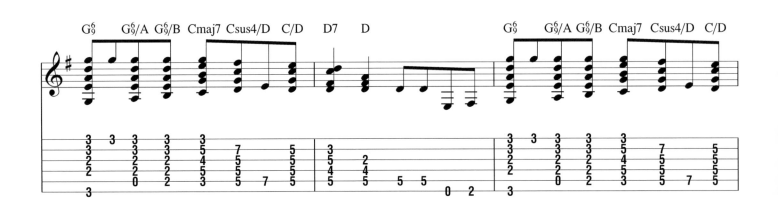

Michelle

Words and Music by John Lennon and Paul McCartney

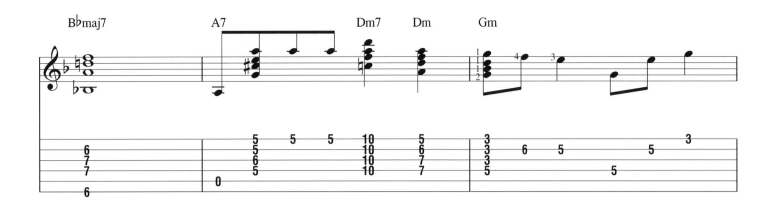

D.S. al Coda

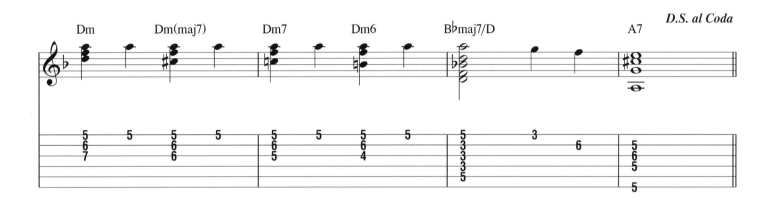

Coda

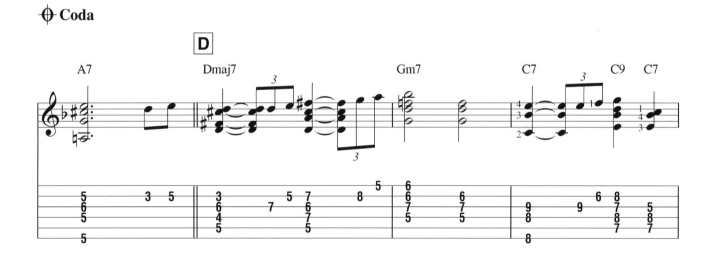

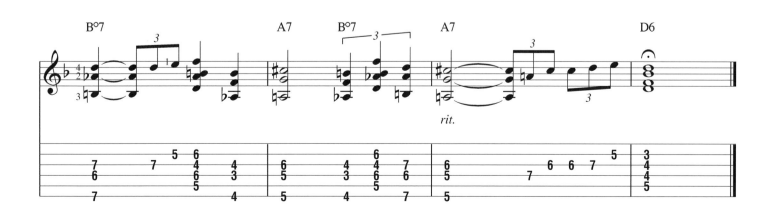

Norwegian Wood

(This Bird Has Flown)

Words and Music by John Lennon and Paul McCartney

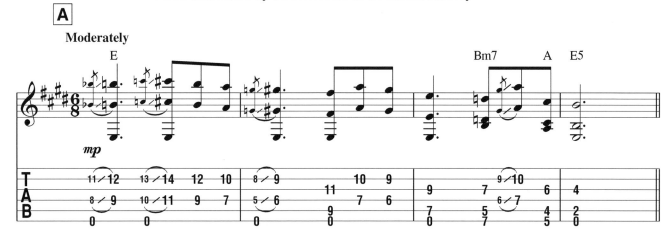

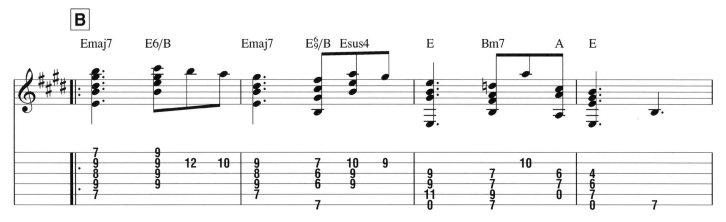

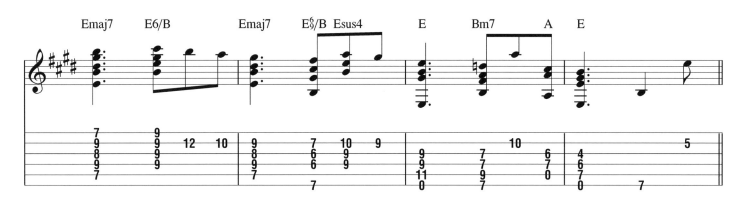

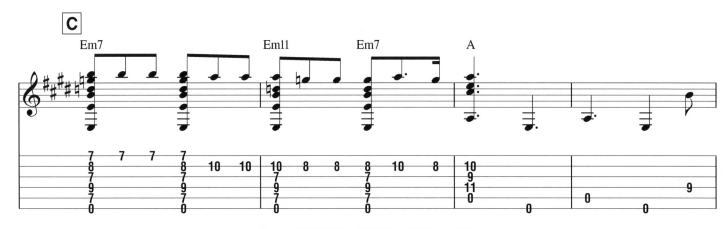

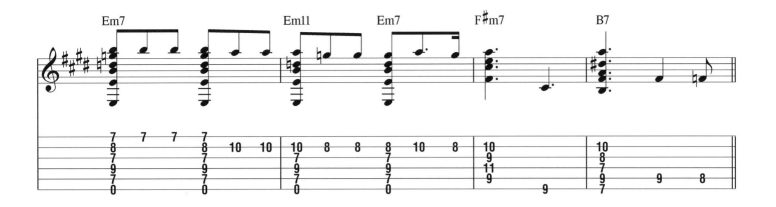

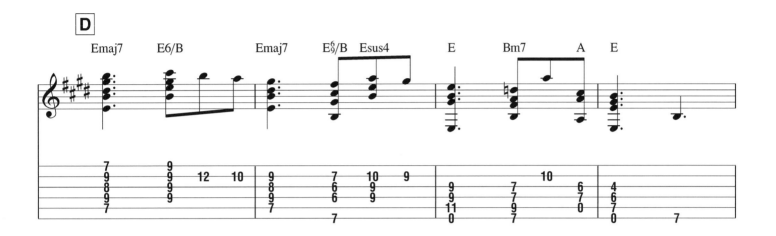

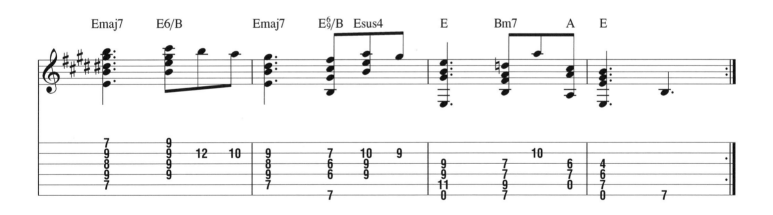

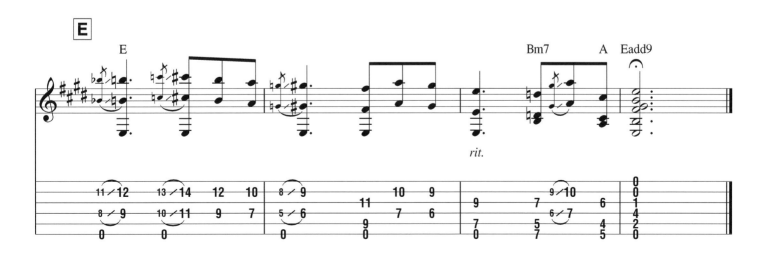

Nowhere Man

Words and Music by John Lennon and Paul McCartney

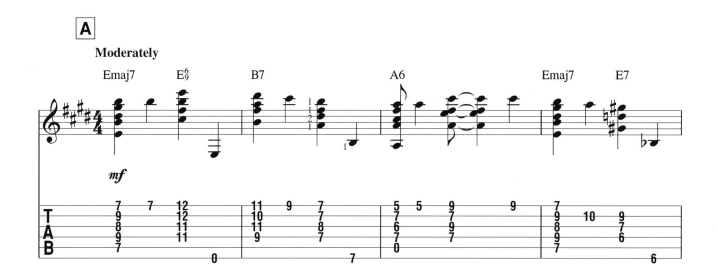

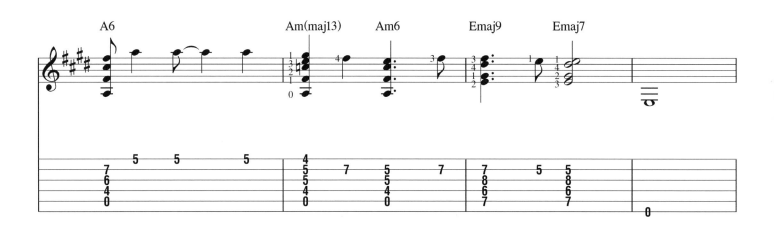

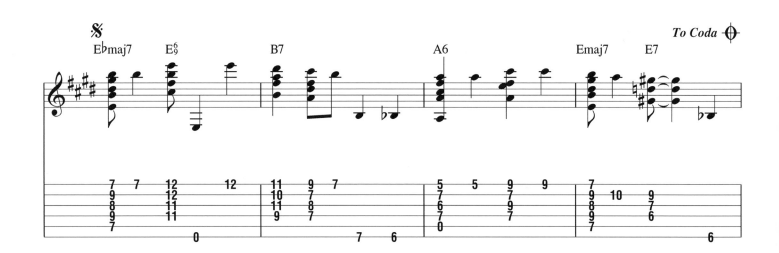

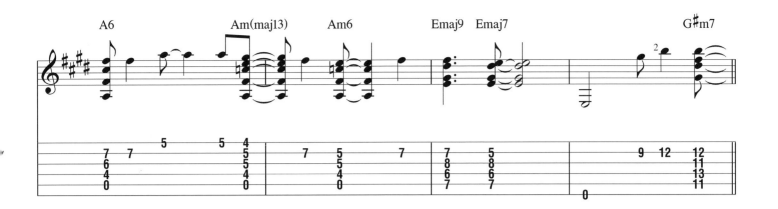

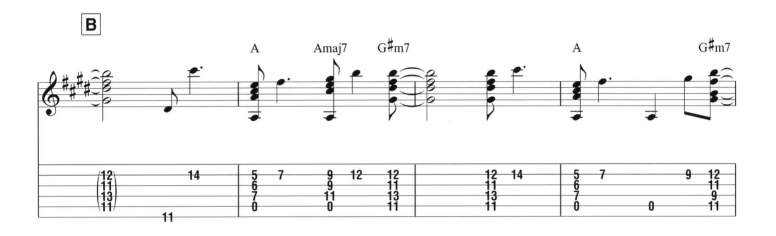

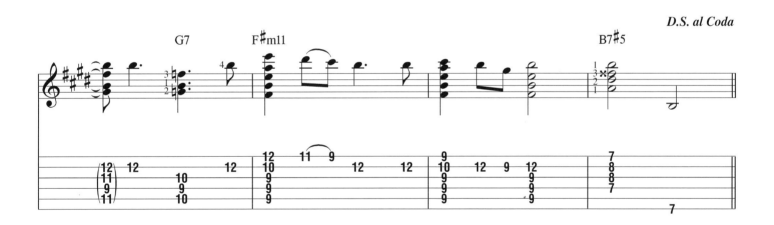

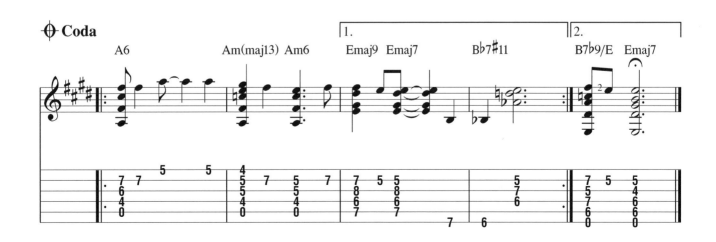

Ob-La-Di, Ob-La-Da

Words and Music by John Lennon and Paul McCartney

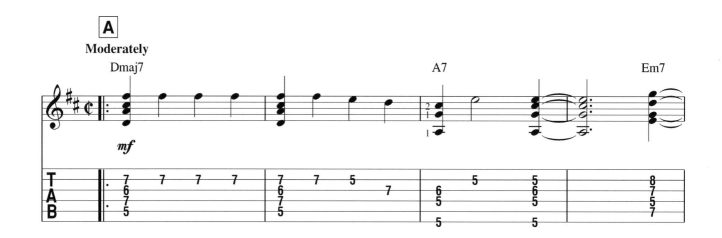

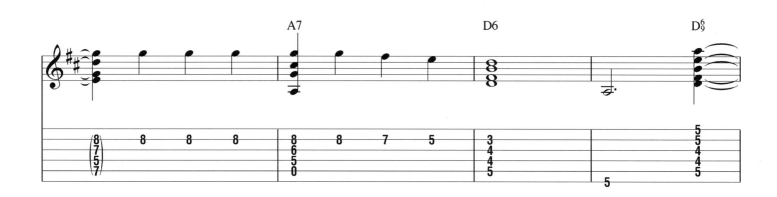

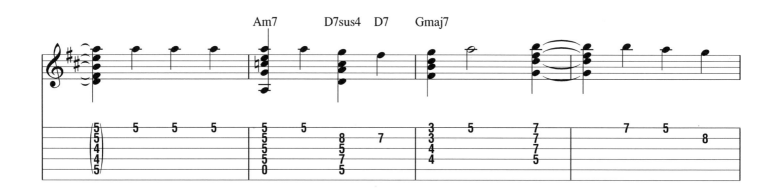

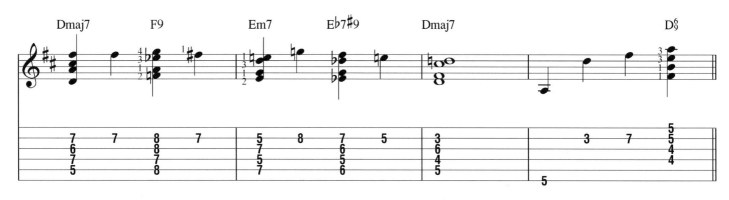

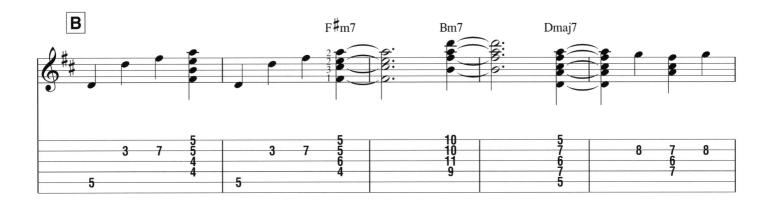

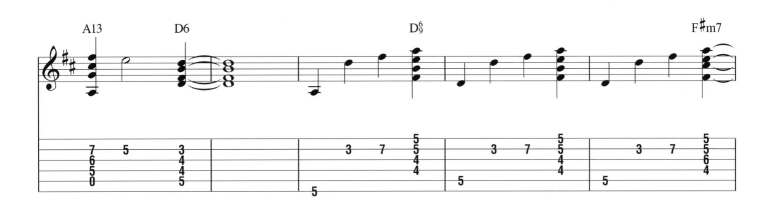

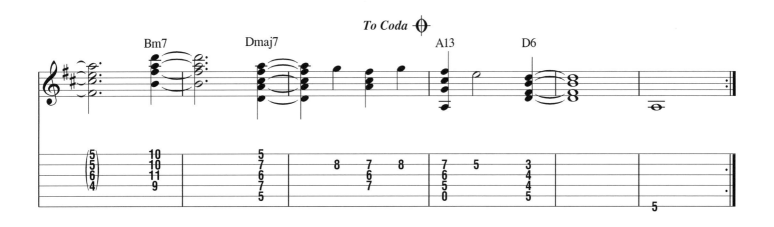

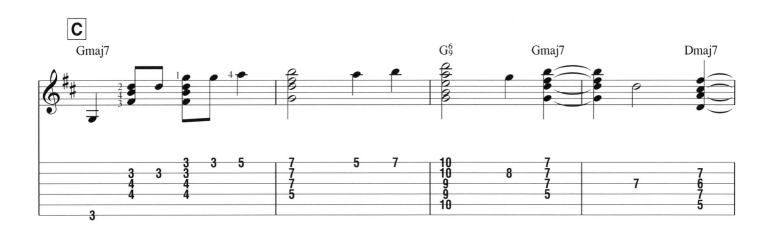

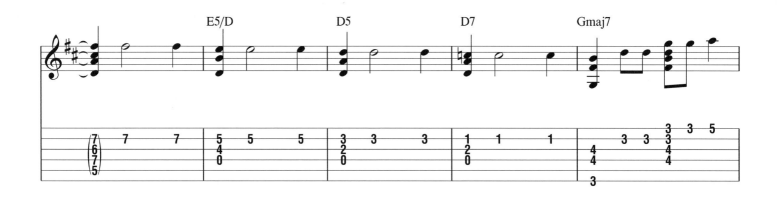

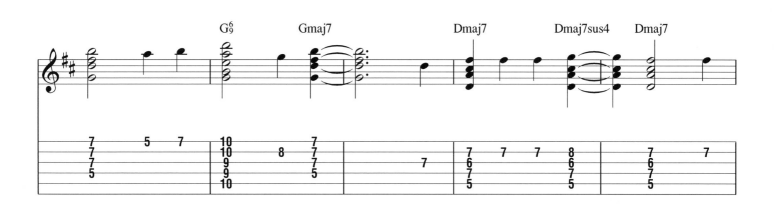

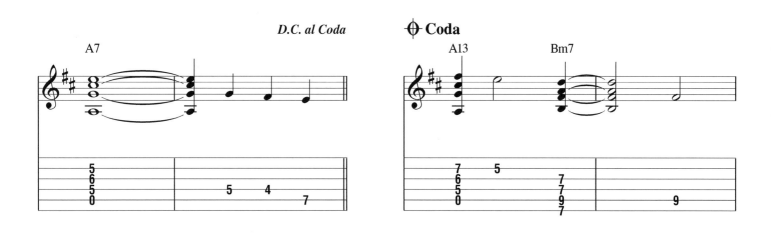

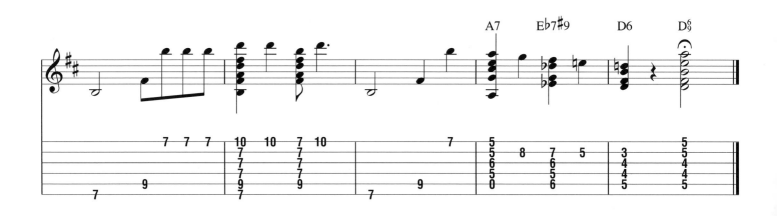

Strawberry Fields Forever

Words and Music by John Lennon and Paul McCartney

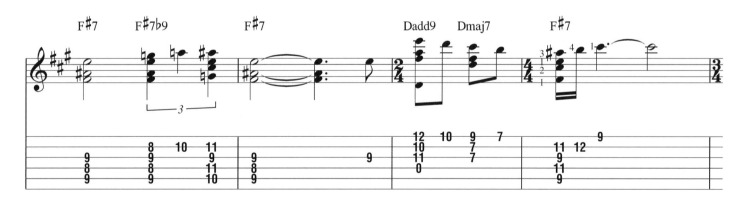

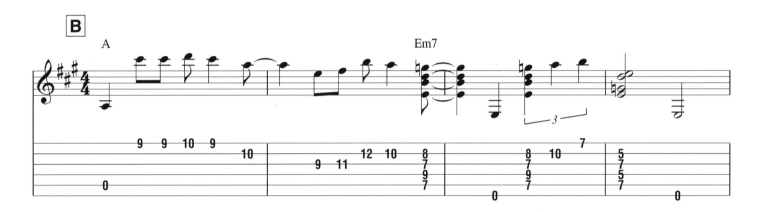

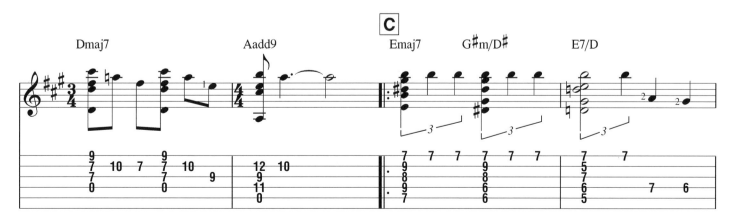

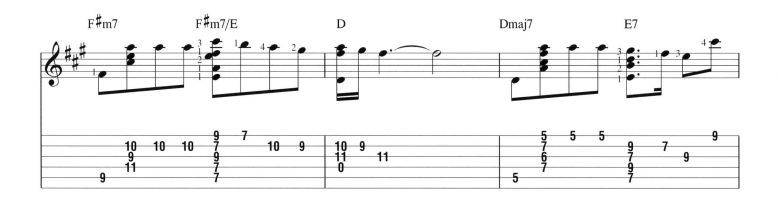

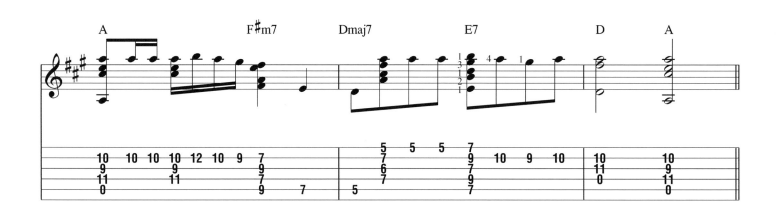

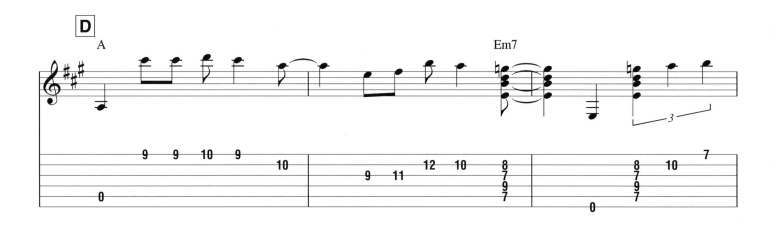

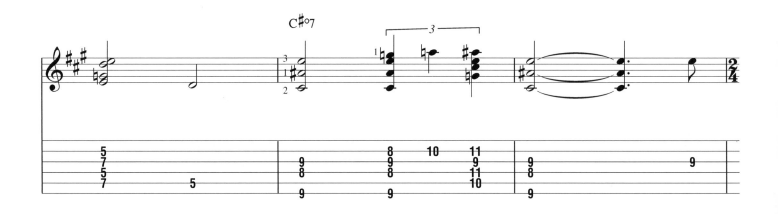

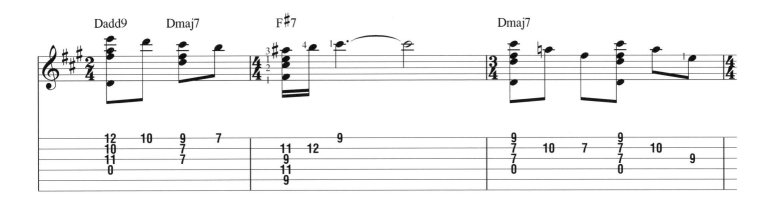

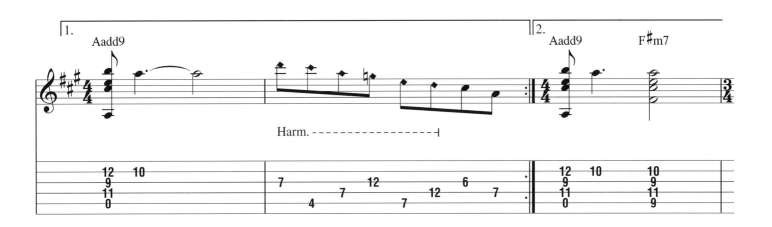

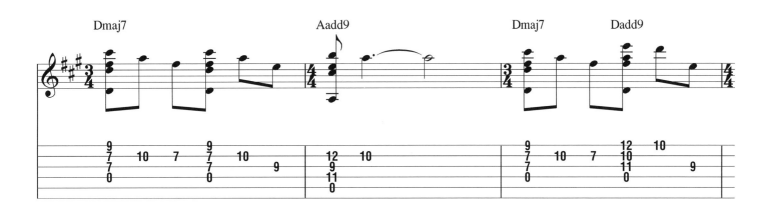

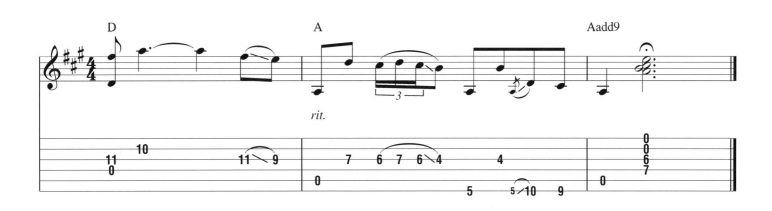

Something

Words and Music by George Harrison

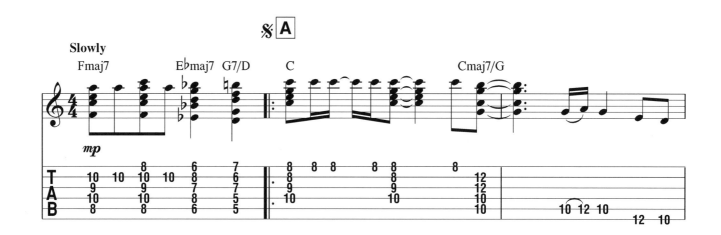

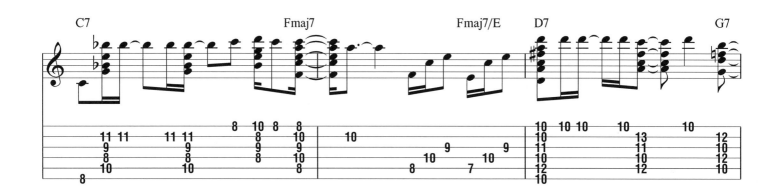

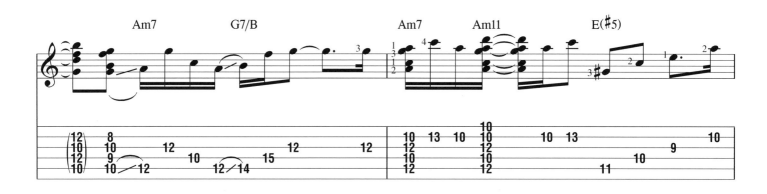

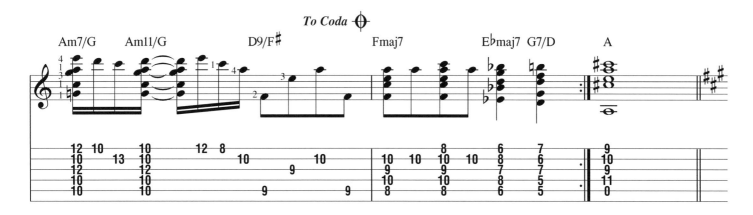

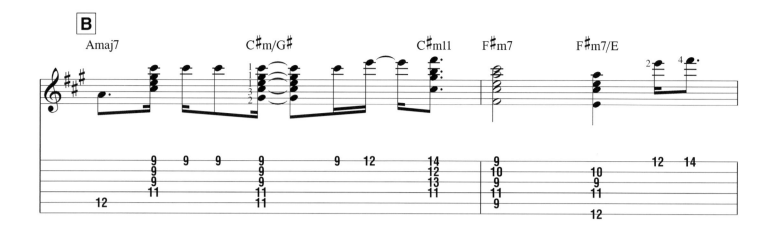

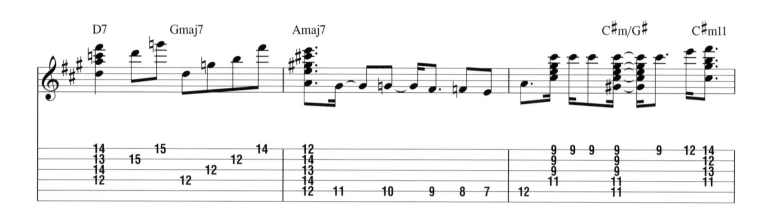

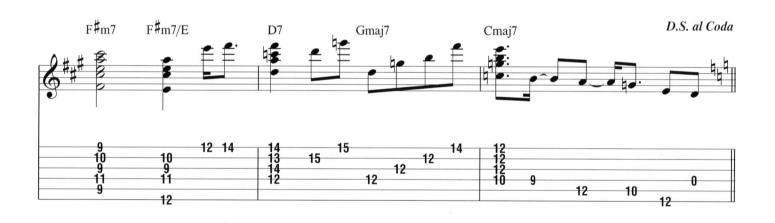

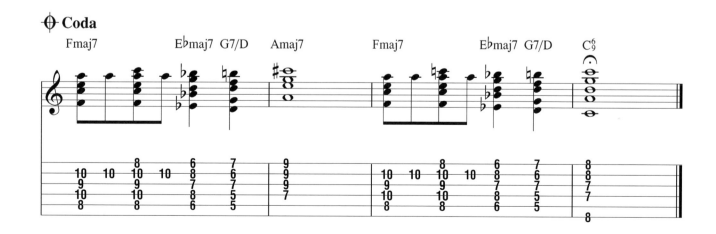

Ticket to Ride

Words and Music by John Lennon and Paul McCartney

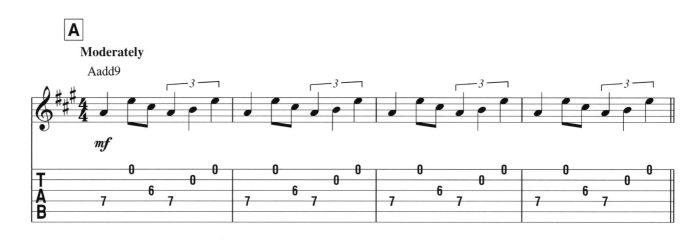

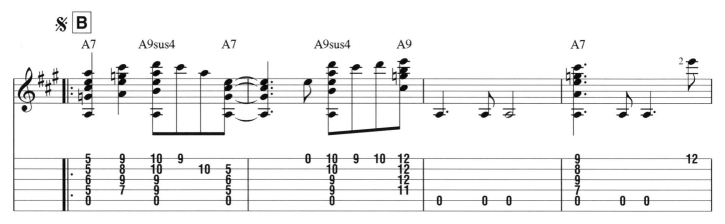

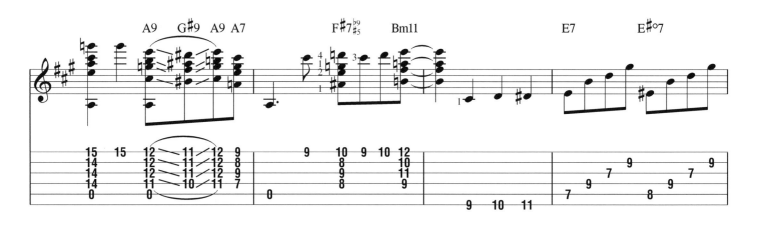

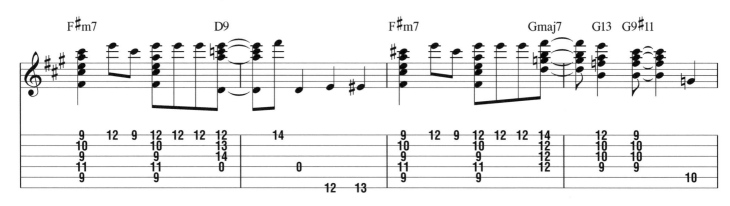

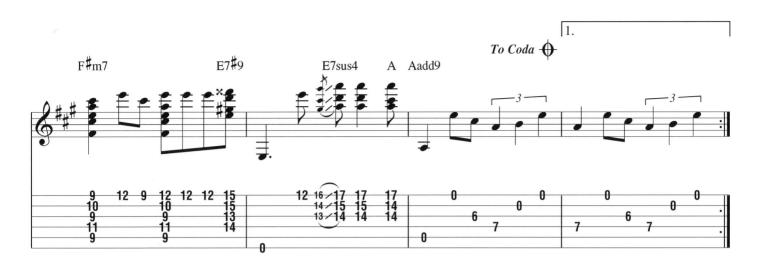

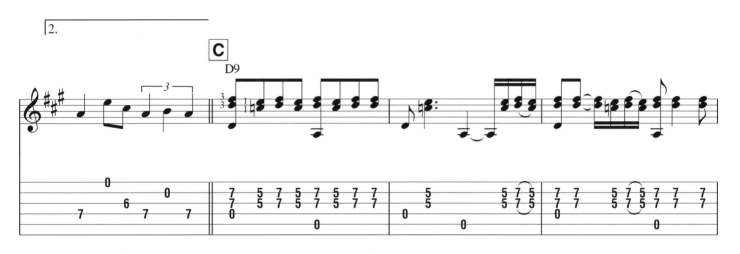

Yesterday

Words and Music by John Lennon and Paul McCartney

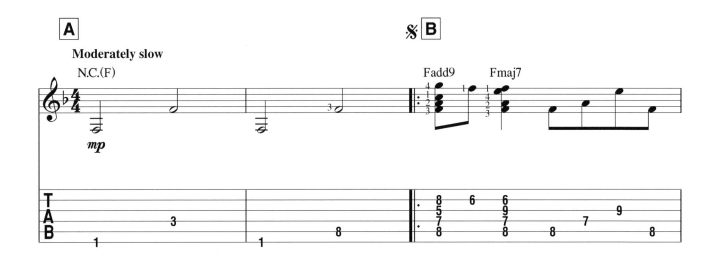

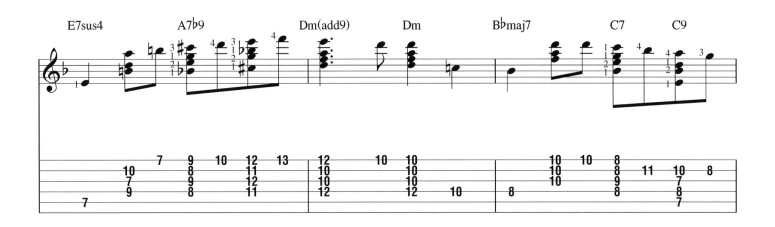

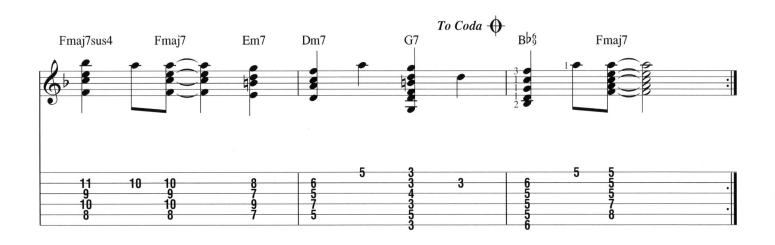

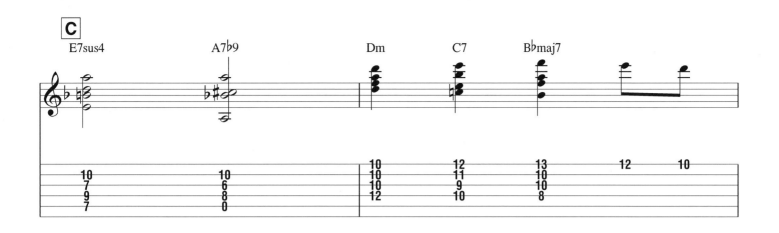

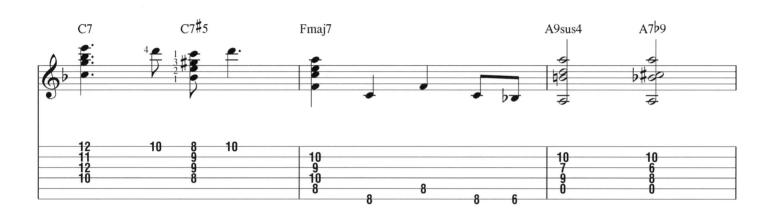

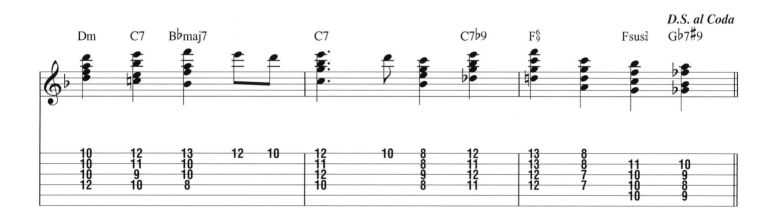

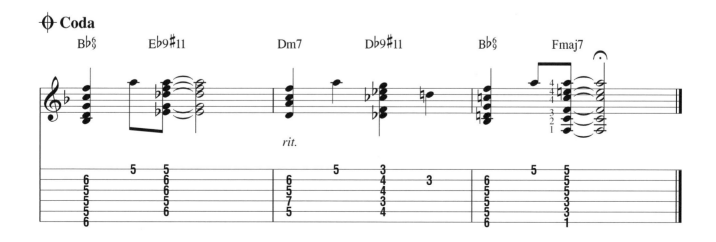

While My Guitar Gently Weeps

Words and Music by George Harrison

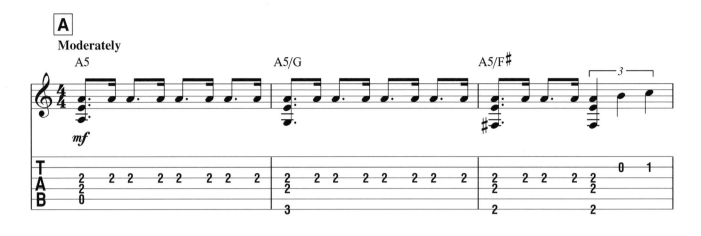

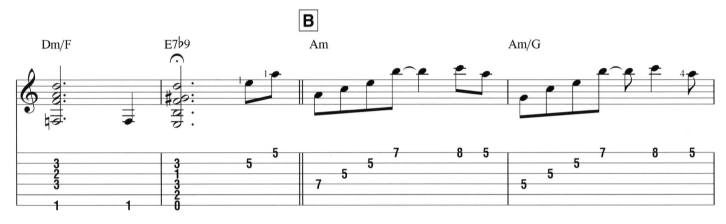

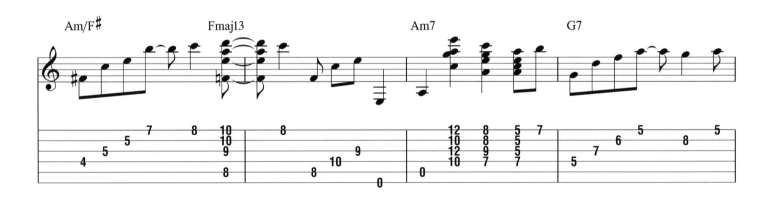

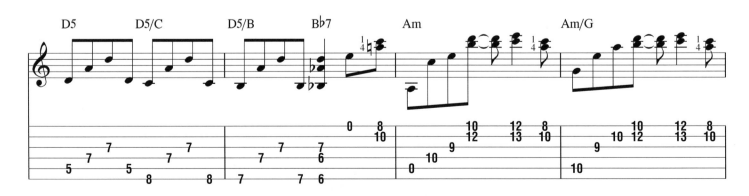

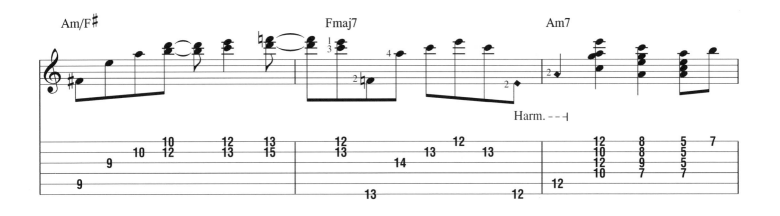

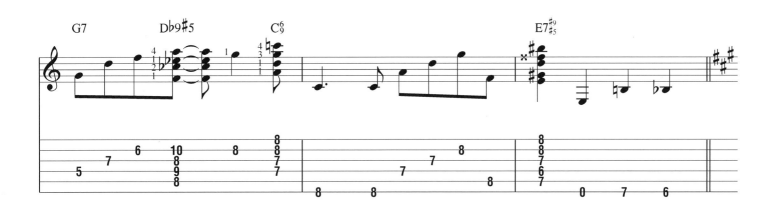

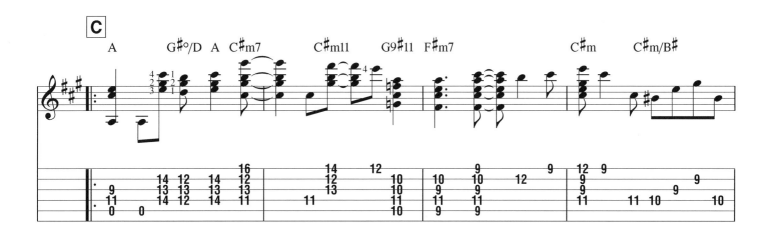

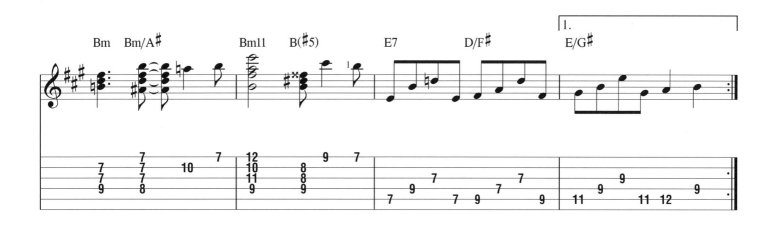

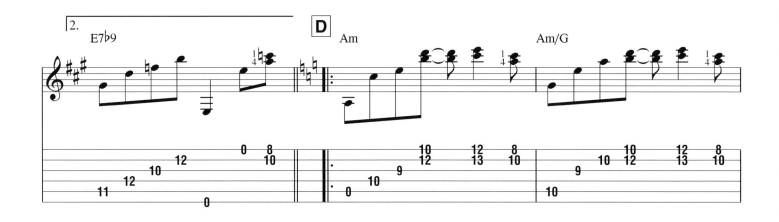

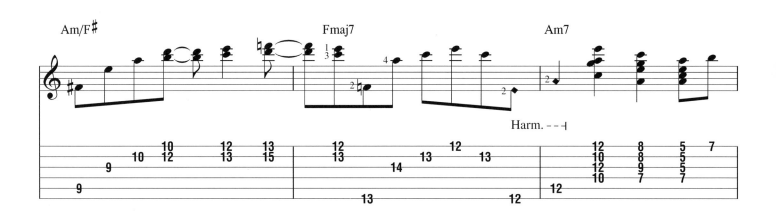

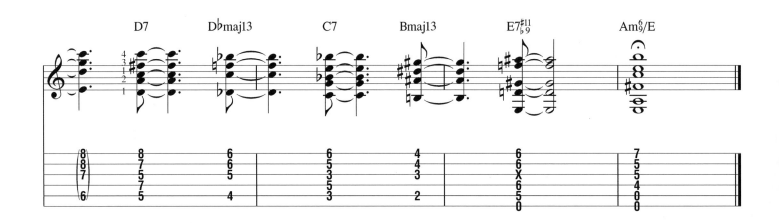

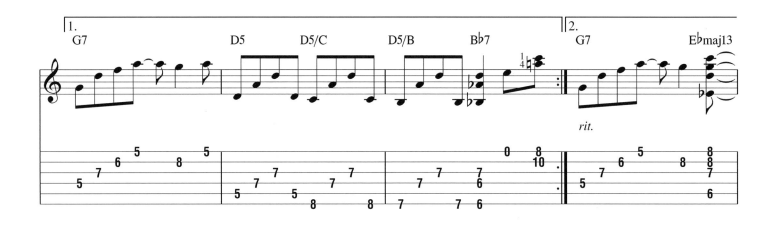